Authentic Leadership

Your Journey to a Five-Star Career

Carey H. Peerman, PhD

Library of Congress Cataloging-in-Publication data

PEERMAN, CAREY H.

Authentic Leadership: Your Journey to a Five-Star Career / by Carey H. Peerman.

p. cm.

Includes biographical references.

ISBN: 978-1-7373745-0-3

Cover design and layout by Karol A. Keane, Keanedesign.com.

Printed in the United States of America

First edition

10 9 8 7 6 5 4 3 2 1

For my family:
My husband, Robert, and son, Thomas
My parents, Glenn and Connie
My sister, Erin
and to all those wonderful leaders,
especially Nancy, who have shaped
my leadership development and believed in me.

And in loving memory of my grandmother,
Lucy Lena' Gregory Atkinson (1911–2008),
with whom I shared a very special bond
and who inspired me from an early age.

To those who keep learning and growing:
"Leadership is a journey not a destination."
—Bill George

Table of Contents

Acknowledgments

Writing my first book has been a wonderful experience. A bucket list item, achieved. I hope there will be more book writing in my future. A project like this takes much time and a group effort to produce. I have many people to thank for assisting me with this endeavor.

My family, particularly my sister, supported me as I worked through many elements of the book's content. My husband and son made my writing time possible and gave me the time I needed to think. I will always be grateful.

A special thank you to Jessica, Deb, Lorraine, and Karol for your expertise and coaching during this process. Your help allowed me to finish this project.

I wish to also thank the many leaders and clients who informed this book. I thank them for their candor in sharing their experiences with me.

Finally, I would like to thank you, the reader. If you are reading this book, you know how important leadership is and how it impacts our daily lives. Thank you for the opportunity to lead you on this journey.

Introduction

To start your journey toward authentic leadership, look first to your past. It is there where you will discover the seeds to your future. What you find may be as simple as the advice given by a teacher or parent, a challenge you overcame—or didn't—or a wish left unfulfilled. It could also be more consequential: a loss or a trauma that has helped you see your path more clearly. In my case, two experiences significantly shaped my path to authentic leadership. One inspired me; the other jolted me into action.

Central to my career as a nurse, nursing home administrator, long-term care consultant, and professor is the time I spent with my Granny. When school let out for the summer, I would stay at her house in the country for several weeks. During this time, we completed cleaning projects, worked in her garden, picked berries, and shared stories over great home-cooked food. From these simple activities, Granny taught me that hard work matters, that nothing is for free, that family is more important than things, and that the kind of person you are is reflected in your work and in how you treat others.

I didn't know it then, but my time spent with Granny would shape my life and career. From my deep love for her came the ability to empathize with and love others. I developed a passion for helping the elderly by advocating for them at their most vulnerable time. From each elderly person I have worked with over the years, I have learned valuable lessons and discovered refreshing perspectives. This passion led to my career in health care and education, where I have led diverse teams, served those needing a high level of care and compassion, and taught emerging leaders.

Not all of the experiences we hold in our past are pleasant, but that doesn't mean we can't learn from them. The second experience that shaped my path to becoming an authentic leader is quite different. It is one of trauma, but it is the one I credit with accelerating my career and setting me on a path to helping others develop the leadership skills needed to work in a health-care setting.

Several years ago, I was involved in an active-shooter event while attending a training conference at a local community college satellite location. An individual with a gun entered the building where training sessions were being held in multiple rooms. When this person began shooting, the sound was so shocking and out of place we couldn't interpret it at first. One person said balloons were popping, and then several responded with the word "gunshots." Our room's door did not lock, so everyone hid as best we could. I remember being terrified and knowing this could be the moment where I met my end.

As I hid, I heard more gunshots, screams, cries for help, and the sound of people scrambling to get out of harm's way. Thoughts about my family and my life streamed through my head. I wanted to see my sweet husband, child, sister, and mother again. My father had passed away several years before, but I felt him with me on that day. I also thought about my unmet goals—the things I'd hoped to achieve but hadn't yet accomplished, either because I hadn't made the effort or hadn't had the opportunity. I understood that I might never have the chance to complete those things.

About that time, I saw the shoes of the gunman near me. All my senses were sharp, and I prayed for more time to live. Then, miraculously, the shoes disappeared. Those fleeting seconds seemed more like hours of thought and discussion in my head, and I vowed that if I made it out alive, I would overcome my fear of change, embrace the future, and achieve my goals.

As part of those resolutions, I decided I would not wait to be shot. I would rather die fighting for my survival than by laying down and waiting. From where I hid, I could see an exit sign. I didn't know if the door would be unlocked or where it would lead. I also didn't know if the gunman was still in the room. What I did know was that I was put on this earth for a reason, and I was going to complete the work I felt called to do. With that knowledge, I got up and went to the door. I knew I might set off an alarm or meet another gunman on the other side, but I was ready to run or fight. With a purposeful push, I opened the door and saw the sunshine of a beautifully clear day on the other side. Seeing a clear path out of the building, I motioned for others to follow. Those who could move ran out of the room. Some were too frightened to move, so others helped them get to safety.

Each person experienced this event differently. Some wet themselves; others lost their shoes; some were disoriented and didn't know their name or could not speak. I helped each person the best I could, trying to reassure them. When the SWAT team arrived, I met them, shared the limited information I had, and guided them to the exit we had used to escape.

The police officers and first responders surrounded the building, ready to do battle and help those inside. Their bravery still gives me goosebumps. As the SWAT team made their way through the building, waves of people were allowed to exit. Finally, a group of officers apprehended the gunman, allowing the emergency responders to carry out the wounded.

Resilient people can improvise, accept reality, and see their lives as meaningful. In the days that followed, I reflected on the active-shooter event and all my thoughts about what I hoped to achieve in life. I had not gotten to choose whether this event happened to me, but I could choose what I did with the experience—and I chose to use it for good, to help myself and others. I was thankful to be alive and knew that my purpose was greater than what I had been doing. I wanted to have a bigger impact on the lives of others, helping them grow and develop the kind of love for others that I had. I decided I could achieve this by transitioning into academia where, as a professor, I could share my knowledge and experience with others through research, writing, and teaching. The fear of change that had kept me from pursuing my goals could not rival the fear I felt in the seconds before deciding to move toward that exit door. Like that decision, I knew my chance was now, and I took the next steps in my career by earning my credential as a fellow of the American College of Healthcare Executives, which allowed me to take the next steps to teach at the college level. I also began networking to find a position that would allow me to work while starting my PhD.

In all of the trauma, I had not forgotten what my Granny taught me about caring for others. True to those lessons, I aimed to earn my doctoral degree in organizational leadership to continue teaching as a professor and to consult for long-term care facilities while continuing my education, a plan that allowed me to satisfy my ambitions while remaining true to my roots.

How to Use This Book

This book will help you on your journey to authentic leadership, encouraging you to reflect on your past self, understand your current situation, and create goals for your future self (see Figure 1). What are the roots of your story? What are your passions? What are your defining moments? A workbook area at the end of Chapters 3, 4, and 5 provides space where you can shape your thoughts and reflections. Take time to explore what gives you the courage to move forward and for what purpose. The answers will keep you focused on what kind of leader you want to be, who you want to lead, and why it matters.

Figure 1

How the Past Self Becomes a Future Leader

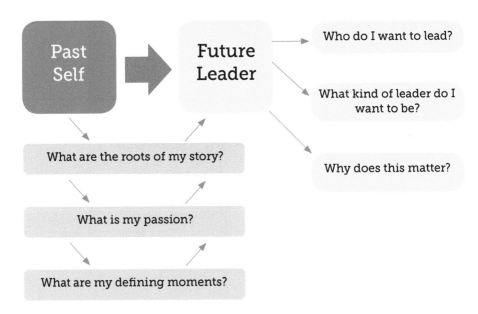

Chapter 1:
Defining Authentic Leadership

Authentic leadership is one of the newer forms of leadership research. In fact, the first discussions of a leader's "authenticity" and "inauthenticity" did not appear until 1983.[1] Since then, the concept of *authentic leadership* has grown from the field of positive organizational behavior, which emerged in 2003.[2] An *authentic leader* has come to be defined as "one who is self-aware of [their] strengths and weaknesses, encourages others' participation and does not impose [their] point of view on others, and acts accordance with personal values, feelings, and beliefs."[3] To me, this means an authentic leader knows who they are, respects others' input, and works to remain true to themself. Leaders derive this kind of authenticity from their past experiences, by learning from successes and failures in a way that informs their leadership style and choices. This willingness to learn makes for leaders who are genuine, directed, and resilient—leaders who know their authentic self.

Why Should You Seek Your Authentic Self?

The theory of authentic leadership continues to evolve, but research has shown people desire leaders who are genuine, honest, and good. The authentic leader develops from experiences or life events that instill a deep sense of conviction about the work they do. Consequently, authentic leadership is something you will develop over your lifetime, perhaps as a practical approach derived from real-life experiences, training, and development. [4,5,6]

As an authentic leader, you can influence your employees and your organization in many positive ways. In today's economy, how employees are engaged and empowered can affect organizational success. Leaders play a critical role in helping organizations reach their goals by creating a climate in which employees are motivated by the positive attitudes and behaviors of others.[7] A positive association exists between employee performance, leadership attitudes, and workplace outcomes. As an authentic leader, therefore, you can significantly nurture and boost employee attitudes, which can lead to a more positive organizational culture.[8]

Authenticity is sought by many but achieved by few. When we see authentic leaders, we are drawn to them and try to understand their motivations, desires, and ways of viewing the world. The journey to establishing yourself as an authentic leader is no easy task and a road not routinely traveled. Growing into an authentic leader takes time, effort, and motivation that is rooted in your passion. On the journey to fully developing yourself as an authentic leader, you will face many challenges and fears that can only be learned as you make your way through the process.

Are You Ready?

So many of us were told as children to follow our dreams. What if we had been told to follow our *passions?* To bring authentic leadership to your workplace, you must conduct a step-by-step review and analysis of your core values and beliefs so you can clearly articulate your passions. Authentic leaders are uniquely positioned to build positive work cultures and create the extraordinary out of the routine. To become an authentic leader, you must:

- Understand your strengths and weaknesses
- Have and act on a defined set of personal values, feelings, and beliefs
- Be an active listener

You also must possess the skills needed to engage others, empower those who feel like they do not have a voice, and boost and nurture employee motivation by building positive attitudes and modeling positive behaviors.

No matter the environment, people want leaders who are genuine and honest, leaders who seek to do good. Doing what is "right" is a foundation for your development as an authentic leader. This kind of leader develops from experiences or life events that instill a deep set of convictions. In my case, my dedication to the elderly grew from the time I spent with my Granny and from my work experiences where I had opportunities to listen to older people talk about their lives and to observe how they chose to live.

Being authentic means developing practical approaches to leadership out of real-life experiences and training—and then applying those approaches to your leadership style in the workplace. You may need to focus on developing yourself as an authentic leader if you have not yet found your niche. This may be true if you answer yes to any of these questions:

- Do you have a strong, unfulfilled desire to feel stable and grounded in your own beliefs, styles, and abilities?
- Do you want to have more of an impact in your workplace or career and feel you lack passion for the work you do?
- Do you want to move forward by using your learned life lessons?
- Do you feel an internal void related to your work that you have not been able to fill?

Some who have chosen to take this journey have benefited from the guidance of great mentors, but at some point, you may have come to a point where you realized you must develop your unique style if you want to one day be the mentor, the coach, the leader you were meant to be. Or perhaps you have found yourself on this journey after realizing the leadership styles defined for you by others don't fit. You identify with the idea of leading with passion or for a cause and know that to do this, you must understand yourself and be able to develop an authentic style to match.

The journey to authentic leadership can take many forms. Still, the overarching reasons for starting the journey are consistent.

- You are uncertain of your style as a leader and want to change that.
- You want to understand what value you can add to your team or organization.
- You want to better understand your uniqueness by defining your passions.
- You want to inspire others and lead your team through challenges and growth.
- You seek a return on your investment, understanding that the more you give, the more you get back.

If you've ever been inspired by an authentic leader, you probably remember them as one you looked up to, as someone who stands out in your past as unique and more respected and well-liked than other managers and authority figures. These kinds of individuals are needed to mentor new leaders, inspire and motivate front-line staff, and promote positive organizational cultures. For you to have this kind of effect, you must know your own story. You must be able to identify your own passions and the values under which they operate. Once you understand where your passions began, you can make a plan for how you want to use these to cultivate a positive work environment for those you lead. You will also be able to draw on this internal grounding to help you connect with followers as they are and form long-lasting compassionate relationships with them. As a well-grounded leader who connects with your followers, you will strengthen engagement, increase empowerment, and cultivate positive attitudes and behaviors.

How Is Authentic Leadership Developed?

Authenticity is believed to be based more in learned values than inherent personality traits. To become an authentic leader, you must begin by connecting with your inner values to understand how they influence your behaviors.[9] Authentic leadership involves four main components:

- Self-awareness
- Internalized moral perspectives
- Balanced information processing
- Relational transparency[10]

Self-Awareness

Self-awareness involves the personal insights leaders have about themselves and how their behavior affects those around them.[11] Self-awareness is the cornerstone to understanding your strengths and weaknesses and the impact you can have on your surroundings. As an authentic leader, you should know your core values, emotions, motives, and goals, and have a strong understanding of who you are and what you stand for.[12] You should also be keenly aware of how these aspects of your identity intersect to formulate your strengths and weaknesses.[13] To lead from your authentic self, you must have achieved a level of self-awareness through which to understand how your identity affects organizational performance.[14]

Internalized Moral Perspectives

Internalized moral perspectives are simply the moral standards you maintain for yourself and others and the extent to which they are influenced by others.[15] Good leaders should have strongly expressed beliefs and morals, and they achieve authenticity when their actions align with those beliefs. When you lead from your authentic self, you will be less susceptible to the external influences of society, other organizations, and your peers.

Balanced Information Processing

Authentic leaders seek others' views, comments, and opinions to explore an issue from all angles.[16] Balanced information processing allows you to take in all information and listen to all perspectives—even those that differ from your own—so you can make an unbiased decision.[17]

Relational Transparency

Relational transparency refers to open and honest communications. Leaders practice relational transparency to ensure others understand their thoughts and motives,[18] which in turn helps them develop dynamic relationships based on trust, cooperation, and teamwork. If you can achieve this level of depth in your established relationships, it will promote growth for both you and your followers.[19]

One way to connect with followers is to be open enough to share some of your life stories. This can help you build trust and find areas of common interest outside of work.[20] Relationships built this way have more potential for growth and are more resilient in the face of pressure and adversity. You can also build relationships by sharing strong, grounded values with others and modeling behaviors based on those values. In this way, these values will become part of who you are and how you perform your work.

Figure 2 illustrates how the concepts in this section come together to form an authentic leader.

Figure 2

Authentic Leadership Model

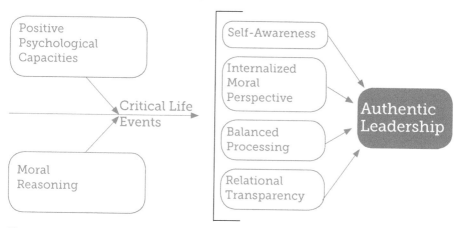

Note. Adapted from Leadership Theory and Practice (6th ed.), by P. G. Northouse, 2013. Copyright 2013 by SAGE.

Chapter 2:
Authentic Leadership as an Antidote

An antidote can be helpful for remedying or neutralizing the effects of certain negative situations. In this case, authentic leadership can either prevent or counteract four critical issues: impostor phenomenon, toxic leadership, professional transition, and ethical collapse.

Impostor Phenomenon
What Is It?
We all know that feeling of not belonging or the feeling of not measuring up to the qualifications for a job. When compounded with learning a new role, these feelings can heighten the fear associated with the impostor phenomenon. Individuals experiencing impostor phenomenon are excessively worried or scared of failure. They are afraid they will not be good enough to carry out their work and will fail. Instead of shying away from this feeling, your journey to being an authentic leader will require you to acknowledge it. Acknowledgment may require a hard look at your actions to see if you are overplanning, overpreparing, and overthinking. In some cases, you may have the false idea that perfection is required.

Once you have identified your version of the imposter phenomenon, you can work to build positive supports to combat it. Positive supports may include focusing on and trusting past wins while identifying and letting go of criticisms that came from individuals from whom you would not seek advice. To overcome impostor phenomenon, you must also adopt an attitude of continuous improvement and growth. This will involve accepting that you do not know everything while remaining willing to learn and acknowledging your ability to do so. As you develop your authentic self, you will learn to identify this phenomenon and see that others often feel the same way. You also may be able to determine the root of the issue and practice positive self-talk that can realign those thoughts. By making a purposeful shift away from the impostor phenomenon you will enter a transitional time to continue working toward the authentic you.

Shared Reflection

While a fairly new administrator, I was asked to make a presentation at a company meeting with corporate leadership and other seasoned administrators in which I would share the different initiatives and projects my facility had been working on. I was new to the company, but had already had a wonderful time improving the services offered to our residents. I enjoyed the opportunity to take an issue and create a unique customer experience that, in turn, led to positive survey results and customer loyalty. Despite my successes, however, I prepared for the meeting to the point of exhaustion. I was fearful that the more experienced administrators and corporate leaders would think our ideas and initiatives were stupid or had already been tried and failed. To my surprise, the presentation went great, and the feedback was overwhelmingly positive. Still, I remained filled with the fear that our work was silly or not good enough. I worried the administrators would expect more good outcomes, and I wasn't sure I could make them happen. What if some of the projects failed? I doubted the praise I'd received was deserved and thought anyone could have accomplished the same. Because I expected perfection, I felt like a failure.

Empathy and genuineness can mix with trust and caring to create an authentic self. Once you've identified your authentic self, you will be a more grounded person who can say, "I belong here," and who can also help others on their journey to being authentic. Becoming an authentic leader in itself marks the resolution of the impostor phenomenon. The fake-it-until-you-make-it strategy becomes unnecessary as you build new relationships and grow into your position.

How Do You Begin?

First, accept that your employer chose you for your position and doesn't expect you to know everything in the beginning. You will develop many skills over time. Individuals seek and need growth; employers realize this and selected you for your ability to grow.

Second, check your "perfection gauge." No one expects you to be perfect, and you shouldn't expect that from yourself either. It is essential to be realistic in setting your personal expectations. Instead, ask yourself, "Did I do my best?"

Third, realize that those feelings of guilt and failure can come from misplaced stress. Find ways to counterbalance any stress you may be carrying.

Fourth, give yourself credit for the excellent work you are doing with each step forward. As they say, Rome was not built in a day. Failures that occur can lead to outstanding successes, so change how you view your failures to see them as pathways to opportunity. Seeing shortcomings as an opportunities is part of developing a growth mindset, a concept discussed further in Chapter 3. With a growth mindset, failure becomes part of the learning process. Without failure, there is no space for improvement and growth.

Fifth, be kind to yourself by developing positive self-talk, using daily affirmations, and accepting that no one is perfect. Developing authentic leadership is an inside-out process that will determine how you handle and overcome the next failure or opportunity.

Toxic Leadership

What Is It?

Individuals are more likely to thrive and do their best work in environments that feel supportive and safe, especially those environments that allow for failure without punishment. Toxic leaders do not create these kinds of environments. Instead, toxic leaders stifle individual growth or organizational success and, in many ways, cause significant harm to the individuals they are supposed to lead. Toxic leaders may be seen as aggressively critical of or otherwise intimidating toward their subordinates. Toxic leaders focus on their own goals and dedicate much of their activity to their own self-interests. This can result can result in narcissistic, abusive, and unpredictable behavior. They tend to make themselves the focus of the work being done over the vision and mission of the organization. They have little to no consideration for their followers' thoughts, ideas, or suggestions. Toxic leaders may demonstrate aggression toward certain employees based on their personality or abilities, especially if an employee has a skill set the leader finds threatening. These destructive actions can have a lasting negative effect on individual followers and organizations. Toxic leaders leave an organization worse than how they found it. They negatively affect organizational culture by reducing follower commitment to the organization, decreasing job satisfaction, producing high turnover, and contributing to followers' negative feelings. Followers may feel like they have been bullied, coerced, or harassed while trying to do their jobs. Unfortunately, toxic leaders can be hard to identify because their followers alone bear the brunt of their behavior. Fear of retaliation and the propensity to transfer departments, leave the company, or be otherwise negatively affected by a toxic leader's misrepresentation of their work or character all hinder a follower's desire and willingness to push back against toxic behavior.

Conversely, authentic leaders promote positive organizational environments, providing the antidote to toxic leadership. Organizations can offset the effects of toxic leaders by instituting checks and balances enabling followers to have a voice and share their concerns. By being an authentic leader, you can be the best answer to toxic leadership, providing followers with encouragement and inspiring them to support and create a positive organizational culture.

Shared Reflection

I have been mostly blessed with leaders who have had my best interests and those of the organization at heart. My experience working with authentic leaders and seeing how they operate has helped me more easily weed out those leaders with negative agendas. However, I have also encountered a few toxic leaders. I have seen leaders stifle employees' input while stealing their ideas, make threats such as "if you're not with me you're against me," and engage in bullying or harrassing behavior such as excluding employees from social events or applying uneven expectations across a team. All of this negative behavior demonstrates how toxicity grows from insecurity. Instead of relying on their own skills and knowledge to shine, toxic leaders undermine their employees to make themselves look superior.

I've also witnessed the extraordinary benefits of substituting authenticity for toxicity. I once experienced a leader who encouraged colleagues to spy on each other and report on observed activities. Who were these employees talking to on the phone? Who had stopped by their office? What were they doing? It appeared this leader hoped to get rid of these individuals or further isolate them from their colleagues. This toxic environment made teamwork almost impossible because trust was lost. Eventually, this leader left the position and was replaced by a new, more positive leader who replaced punitive actions with a collaborative approach; this leader asked for input, too, which made followers feel valued. The change led to a growing culture of trust and a positive work environment where people thrived and engaged rather than feeling perpetually deflated.

How Do You Begin?

First, recognize when you have a toxic leader. Identifying a toxic leader is not about blaming a leader for your shortcomings, but rather understanding how the leader treats you. Toxic leaders can cause irrevocable damage to an organization and to employees by hindering performance and creating unnecessary stress.

Second, know how to make the most of a bad situation. Learn to neutralize your toxic leader's behavior by setting boundaries and distancing yourself while still maintaining respect. If the toxic leader makes you feel under constant surveillance, be flexible, competent, and transparent in your communications. If the toxic leader needs to feel their power, support them with praise and credit, and choose your battles wisely.

Third, decide if you want to stay and wait for the toxic leader to move on or if you want to find a new position. Many times, toxic leaders move on abruptly, either from their need for a new challenge or from illness. I have personally seen how all of that negative energy can take a physical toll on a leader's health. If you decide to leave, continue to use your skills to maintain your position while carefully looking for a new position in an organization you can support. Seek an organization that has implemented practices that make toxic leadership impossible.

Fourth, experiencing a toxic leader can help your growth as an authentic leader. Seeing and experiencing first-hand the different ways leaders behave and treat others will help you on your journey to authentic leadership by clearly demonstrating for you the kind of leader you do and do not want to be.

Professional Transition
What Is It?
All leaders have experienced a point in their career—or several!—where they have needed and wanted to become more authentic as a leader. Each of these points of transition represents a fork in the road where you can learn more about your authentic self. Finding yourself in a new territory or uncomfortable in your current environment, you may feel uneasy about the self-growth that often occurs during these times. Examples of this kind of professional transition include when you: (a) first graduate from college, (b) transition from follower to leader, (c) have been mentored or coached by a leader who no longer fits your developing leadership style, or (d) have evolved your leadership skills with one organization to the point that you no longer fit the organization's mission and vision.

The professional transition from college student to working professional can be a challenge. It is crucial to stay connected to your network during this time because this is where you often find your first employment opportunities. If you feel you need to strengthen your network, you can attend job fairs, trade shows, and professional organizations aligned with your field. Always dress for success, be willing to go the extra mile to gain new skills or experiences, and keep business cards on hand.

When you transition from follower to leader, you must build on your past experiences, passions, and authentic self. This transition can make or break you as a leader. As you shift from peer to leader, you should expect growing pains and learning curves. As a new leader, you must understand your organization and the expectations of your new leadership position, and you must have the ability to carry out the work tasks while inspiring a team and allowing for self-growth. In this new role, the ability to understand, direct, and manage your own emotions (i.e., your *emotional intelligence*) will significantly assist you in developing your authentic leadership. Ways to improve your emotional intelligence go beyond this book's scope, but these skills will enhance your leadership journey, so if this is an area where you feel you need improvement, see the work of Daniel Goleman, especially "What Makes a Leader," or *Emotional Intelligence 2.0*, by Travis Bradberry and Jean Greaves. In addition to knowing yourself, get to know your team members and their unique strengths, learn how to listen to them, and be willing to think outside the box and take action.

There are times in our careers when we have the opportunity to receive mentoring or coaching related to advanced leadership roles. Mentors and coaches are seasoned leaders who want to give back to their profession by helping less seasoned individuals gain skills and abilities. Such relationships often last a lifetime and can be mutually beneficial. However, there are also times when individuals grow apart from their mentor or coach. I have seen this occur when, as part of authentic leadership development, leaders have asked mentees to take actions or grow in a direction outside their authentic morals, values, and self-expectations. When these rooted differences surface, your commitment to authenticity will require that you change directions and leave this relationship on the highest note possible.

When your leadership growth with one organization evolves to the point that you no longer fit the organization's mission and vision, you must prepare for a professional transition. This type of authentic growth happens more often than you may think. I often hear colleagues talking about not being "in tune" or "on board" with what their organization is trying to accomplish. I've heard others lament being asked to carry out work that conflicts with their beliefs. In your own career, you may have heard these complaints or may have heard a colleague comment that "this position is not what I signed up for," or "I can't believe how much the organization has changed," or "this job is different because the company is no longer the same." If you experience such revelations yourself, you should recognize them as cues that your authentic self no longer aligns with the organization.

How Do You Begin?

These professional transition moments can be challenging, but they also provide opportunities for you to develop your authentic self and align your authentic leadership style with your professional career.

First, recognize that you are in a state of professional transition. As previously discussed, several different scenarios indicate the evolution of your authentic self. Embrace this realization and use it to guide your transition.

Second, developing authentically as a leader is no easy journey. You may feel uncomfortable and unsure, but this will pass as you reaffirm your goals, morals, and values and establish a new direction. For growth to occur, you need to be open to the new journey, be vulnerable as you transform, and be able to connect with others. Your authentic self is often what remains when you stop trying to impress others and instead lead with your heart and passion.

Third, expand your network to find your next career opportunity. Going through a professional transition can lead to a new career that is more in line with your authentic self.

Fourth, seek a mentor who can inspire and help you cultivate the authenticity you have developed. This mentor should be able to help you grow in a new direction.

Ethical Collapse

What Is It?

Authentic leaders encounter daily challenges to their commitment to lead with the character and morals that will provide a solid foundation for the ethical organization. Ethics will play a large role in your leadership decisions while also influencing your followers and your industry. In most cases, unethical organizations are alike: their cultures are identical, and their inevitable collapses are predictable. A pattern appears to exist that can predict the impending failure of unethical organizations. It begins with the pressure to compete. Then an employee discovers a flaw in the process or product and reports the concern. The management team does not want to hear bad news, so they hide the issue, ultimately hurting the customer. The organization becomes at risk of ethical collapse, and failure becomes imminent. As an authentic leader, you will be well equipped to guard against this predictable pattern because your leadership decisions are based on high moral principles. You will also have established solid relationships with your followers by engaging them in open and honest ways.

All authentic leaders require an in-depth understanding of how politics, power, and ethics influence organizational culture. Leadership and the nature of business operations cause ethical dilemmas. Being an authentic leader means you must acknowledge and understand the moral implications of decisions made and how those decisions affect others in the organization. Leaders must set and maintain an ethical business culture. As an authentic leader, you will be best able to meet this call because of your previous work ensuring your moral perspectives align with the organization's mission and ethics. But there's more to it than that: As an authentic leader, you must also commit to hearing all views and perspectives while ultimately ensuring that all decisions align with the organization's goals and your moral perspectives. This focus will help you build a trusting relationship with your followers, strengthening the ethical landscape in which they operate. As an authentic leader, you should adopt

Shared Reflection

Ethics and values can vary significantly among groups and organizations. In my career, I have served in very ethical and compliance-oriented organizations. In ethically driven organizations, employees are free to question policies and procedures and actions of colleagues or leaders without retaliation. I have brought ethical or compliance concerns to committees for review and clarification. The outcomes were addressed with clarification and additional education. I was never punished or retaliated against. Instead, I was thanked for sharing my view. As authentic leaders, we must remember that doing the right thing is at our core—and, in some cases, to achieve this we must bring issues of concern forward. This can be hard to do when voicing a concern could cost you your job. As an authentic leader, you must keep the big picture in mind and those you serve in your heart because these things will give you the courage to do what is right.

a positive outlook on life and value truthful and transparent interactions with your followers. In this way, you will enhance team performance by setting high ethical standards and garnering trusting followers who value their teams' work outcomes.

How Do You Begin?

First, be rooted in your morals, values, and ethical compass. Have a clear understanding of what is right and what is wrong. Explore what-ifs that may be unethical so you can rationalize the concepts and develop internal triggers to warn you of a potential violation.

Second, research an organization before you join the team. Are they ethical? Do they have checks and balances in place to keep ethics a priority? Have lawsuits been filed against them that trigger your moral compass? You will need to make a judgment call about whether you want to be associated with this organization. Are you willing to represent this organization using your good name?

Third, does the organization have an ethics or compliance committee? Are employees encouraged to report suspected violations or concerns? Are there clear policies and procedures to help guide the overall functions of the organization? Some industries, such as health care and education, are more regulated than others. As a potential employee in a more regulated industry, you can often determine if there is an ethics or compliance committee from the organizational chart. Is there a legal team or a compliance officer position? When touring the organization, do you see hotline compliance numbers posted? You can also ask about other means of providing feedback such as employee satisfaction surveys, a suggestion box, or open discussion forums. Remember that you have every right to ask about the types of ethics and compliance committees that support an organization during an interview.

Fourth, as an authentic leader, you must be fearless in your approach to ethical concerns or violations. You must be willing to do what is right no matter the personal cost to yourself.

Chapter 3:
The Authentic Leader's Journey

Becoming an authentic leader takes time and effort. To get there, you must embark on a continuous journey of self-discovery, self-improvement, reflection, and renewal.[21,22] You must acknowledge your leadership style, personality, and values regardless of situational factors. As an authentic leader, you have the power to transform an organization's work environment into one of happiness, laughter, productivity, and continued growth. Employees who work for authentic leaders report having a sense of family at their workplace, which indicates a healthy work environment. The key to a successful organization is to have empowered, authentic leaders at all levels who can inspire, develop, and create change through others.[23] This is why authentic leadership should be developed purposefully. Healthy work environments are characterized by trust between management and employees. Employees in these environments actively engage in their work, have a voice in decision making, take innovative risks, feel empowered, and seek professional growth.

Self-Reflection: *Ask yourself*

Does this organization align with my passion?

Is my leadership example inspiring others?

What are my potential growth areas?

Self-Discovery and Self-Improvement

Developing authenticity is no easy task, but you can achieve it through persistence and determination. You must be honest with yourself and focus on your passions. Authentic leaders are intentional about their work to cultivate their passion and promote growth. To do this, you must understand your overall goals and how they relate to the things that matter to you. In some cases, these factors may also tie into the organization's goals as leaders drive them.

Three main strengths stand out for authentic leaders:

- Their actions are real and genuine.
- They accept and care for others, respecting where others are in their own journey and understanding where their followers' growth may lead.
- They express empathetic and compassionate understanding that benefits the team and themselves.

Real and Genuine Action

Authentic leaders do the right thing for the right reason, help others, and support followers' growth. As an authentic leader, you will lead by example. By doing so, you will create a great sense of motivation, inspiration, and vision for others to follow. Authentic leaders are resilient people. They possess emotional intelligence and agility, which are key attributes of authentic leaders. Emotional intelligence is linked to individual self-awareness, self-regulation, motivation, social skills, and empathy. Leaders with high emotional intelligence can control their emotions and understand how their behavior affects others. This might translate into a situation where leaders are aware of their followers' emotional well-being, which can be useful when managing challenging situations. *Emotional agility*, on the other hand, refers to the ability to use negative experiences

Self-Reflection: *Ask yourself*

Am I emotionally intelligent?

What skills need development?

22

for good. This ability allows the leader to experience their world and thoughts positively.

Emotionally intelligent and agile leaders help organizations drive innovation and efficiency and manage change. Leaders with these abilities will be able to cope with difficult scenarios through real and genuine action that is not driven by emotions alone. The emotionally intelligent and agile leader helps create a path toward growth for the individuals and organizations involved.

Shared Reflection

I have witnessed leaders transition from yelling, screaming, hot-headed bullies to leaders with emotional intelligence able to further the goals of the organization. In particular, I knew a leader with great business skills but no people skills. This leader yelled at subordinates, talked down to them, and belittled them. Some followers found a way to tolerate this inappropriate behavior and remain on the job while others quickly left the organization. This leader quickly figured out that his emotional outbursts were hurting his team. He also came to see that those leaving perceived him as a hot-headed monster.

Instead of digging in his heels, this leader engaged in self-reflection and hired a leadership coach. Over time, he developed his emotional intelligence and transformed himself into a better listener who others wanted to be around. He remains in his position and is now viewed as a leader that others want to follow.

Care for Individuals

Authentic leaders have influence their organizations in multiple ways. If you lead authentically, you will experience increased job satisfaction, high performance levels, and longevity in your job.[24] These same effects will be mirrored in your followers because they feel happy, fulfilled, supported, encouraged, and nurtured in ways that exceed their individual expectations.

Authentic leaders can also be great mentors and coaches who are clear about creating a vision for others' achievement. The ability to help others develop an achievement plan comes from the authentic leader's strong sense of self. Their concepts of self are organized and consistent.

Empathy for Others

The authentic leader's ability to feel and show empathy in the workplace allows for genuineness and authenticity. Empathy involves the leader's ability to relate to another person's shared verbal feelings or feelings that are intuitively understood. Empathy helps one connect with others on many different levels. It is a strong tool that can tune leaders into the subtleties of body language and the messages between spoken words. Empathetic leaders will also be keenly aware of followers' cultural and ethnic differences that may affect these employees' workplace expectations and values. Empathy also plays a key role in the retention of followers.

Shared Reflection

One of my employees once came to work and shared they had been up all night with a family member who was sick and in the hospital. I empathized. I have also lost sleep due to family illness or crisis, so I knew how they felt, how their heart hurt and their brain felt foggy from lack of sleep. I drew on my empathy to help guide my response. I told them how sorry I was and that I understood if they needed to go home to rest or be with their family. I gave them the freedom to choose what was best for them as a person, showing them I cared about them and was willing to support them in their time of need. Trust already characterized our relationship, and my response validated that. My employee responded with loyalty and reliability. We always knew we could count on each other.

Unconditional positive regard allows the authentic leader to guide followers to a better path because they feel cared about, individually. This approach allows authentic leaders to instill deep trust and loyalty while establishing a caring environment where individuals flourish, and the organization reaps the rewards.

Self-Reflection: *Ask yourself*

Am I empathetic toward others?

Can I identify instances where empathy informed my leadership decisions?

Can I identify instances where I could have been more empathetic? How would empathy have changed my decisions?

Are there relationships I would like to strengthen?

Expressions of empathy and genuine, unconditional positive regard strengthen teams, so authentic leaders are predisposed to teambuilding because their leadership style relies on these qualities. Because authentic leaders understand the benefits of having and developing a great team, team collaboration becomes a focal point as they groom each team member for their own position in counterbalance with the skills, talents, and abilities of others on the team. Through empathy, authentic leaders build teams out of relationships that will last a lifetime.

Shared Reflection

Have you ever worked with a leader who is just a really great person? I have , and the experience was one of great learning and self-reflection. I met this leader when I transitioned into her role as she moved on to another opportunity. I immediately learned that she was real and genuine. She helped me grow in ways that helped me be a better leader. She wanted what was right for everyone—peers and followers alike.

Emotional intelligence and (especially) empathy were her strengths. She led with her heart and used her mind to keep her perspective, as an authentic leader should. She could take a bad situation and reach a positive outcome for everyone. In one example, when an employee didn't follow through on a client request, she expressed understanding about what it feels like to make an error. Then she guided the employee in their effort to rectify the situation with the client. In the end, the employee felt empowerd; the client was pleased with the resolution; and the leader solved the problem without imposing punishment, retribution, or shame.

This leader's expressions of care and respect allowed her followers to see how they could make a situation right and helped them see how they could turn a negative event into a positive one for all involved. She helped others around her to grow in a variety of ways and mentored others to help them become a better version of themselves. No matter what, she saw the good in the person before her.

Exploring Your Past to Shape Your Present

We have discussed the main strengths of authentic leadership. We have also acknowledged that everyone has negative experiences in our pasts that we could turn into positives. For me, the active shooter event was an extreme example. You may have experienced the loss of a loved one, a divorce, a job loss, or another great disappointment. What differs among us isn't whether we've experienced disappointment, loss, or fear, but how we respond to these things when they occur. The active-shooter event I experienced will always be a defining moment in my life. The choice of what to do with that experience was mine, and I chose to build something positive out of it. Your past experiences can help you create a sense of self-actualization that defines who you are as a leader. How will your past shape your authentic self?

What positive or negative past experiences have made me stronger? Why?

What did I learn from those experiences that I didn't know before?

What lessons have I brought with me (or could I bring) from the past into my present life?

Which past experiences do I wish I'd handled differently?

How can the things I'm learning from my past experiences affect my future behavior and decisions?

Exploring Gifts and Mindfulness

To become authentic, you must identify your gifts and talents. You can also learn from watching and observing others as they experience positive and negative reinforcements. Understanding how and why other leaders earn recognition and rewards can guide your leadership development. Additionally, watching and observing an authentic leader can help mold your actions and responses and help you think about how you might choose to do things differently.

What are my gifts and talents?

How can these strengthen me as an authentic leader?

Authentic leaders use mindfulness to connect with themselves, others, and the larger community. *Mindfulness* refers to your basic human ability to be fully present in your thoughts, feelings, bodily sensations, and surrounding environment. Being mindful allows leaders to initiate or guide change skillfully. Mindfulness practice can improve focus, clarity, creativity, and compassion.[25] It can also help you overcome attachment, aversion, ignorance, confusion, delusion, envy, jealousy, and pride.

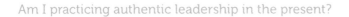

Growth Mindset

To bring all of this together, you must have a growth mindset and motivate followers to do the same. Inidividuals with a growth mindset see challenges and obstacles as opportunities to learn and grow. Genetics determine intelligence, but an openness to learn also plays a role. Brain development continues throughout our lives. Modeling a willingness to learn when you or your team encounter challenges and showing your followers you care about their continuing development can help them open their own minds and motivate them to reach a higher level of personal development.

Individuals with a growth mindset accept failure as a part of learning. You may have experienced demoralizing thoughts such as: *I can't do this. This doesn't work. I don't know. It doesn't make sense. I don't get it. I'm not good at this.* To adopt a growth mindset, add the word "yet" to the end of each of these thoughts. As an authentic leader, you can promote your own learning and that of your followers—and transform everyone's abilities.

What did I do today that made me think?

What occurred today that made me want to keep going?

What is the take-away lesson?

What error did I make that I learned from today?

What efforts made me feel stretched today?

How am I going to adapt my efforts for better results?

What obstacles and opportunities did I encounter today?

What will I do to help myself improve and grow?

Alignment with the organization
Does this organization align with your passion?

_____

_____

_____

Is your leadership example inspiring others?

_____

_____

_____

What are your potential growth areas?

_____

_____

_____

Emotional intelligence
Are you emotionally intelligent?

_____

_____

_____

What skills need development?

_____

_____

_____

Mentoring skills
Are you ready to be a coach or mentor to your followers?

_____

_____

_____

What skills could you improve?

_____

_____

_____

Empathy
Are you empathetic toward others?

_____

_____

_____

Can you identify instances where empathy informed your leadership decisions?

_____

_____

_____

Can you identify instances where you could have been more empathetic? How would empathy have changed your decisions?

_____

_____

_____

Are there relationships you would like to strengthen?

_____

_____

_____

Reflecting on past experiences
What positive or negative past experiences have made you stronger? Why?

_____

_____

_____

What did you learn from those experiences that you didn't know before?

_____

_____

_____

What lessons have you brought with you (or could you bring) from the past into your present life?

_____

_____

_____

Which past experiences do you wish you'd handled differently?

_____

_____

_____

How can the things you're learning from your past experiences affect your future behavior and decisions?

_____

_____

_____

Identifying gifts and talents
What are your gifts and talents?

_____

_____

_____

How can these strengthen you as an authentic leader?

_____

_____

_____

Mindfulness

Are you practicing authentic leadership in the present?

_____

_____

_____

Are there times when you let yourself be distracted by past events or worries about what's to come?

_____

_____

_____

Can you focus more on the present? How can you do so to achieve current goals?

_____

_____

_____

Growth mindset

What did you do today that made you think?

_____

_____

_____

What occurred today that made you want to keep going?

_____

_____

_____

What is the take-away lesson?

_____

_____

_____

What error did you make that you learned from today?

_____

_____

_____

What efforts made you feel stretched today?

_____

_____

_____

How are you going to adapt your efforts for better results?

_____

_____

_____

What obstacles and opportunities did you encounter today?

_____

_____

_____

What will you do to help yourself improve and grow?

_____

_____

_____

Chapter 4:
Authentic Leadership and Your Career

Reinventing yourself as an authentic leader means redefining your habits, routines, roles, and responsibilities in ways that can apply to your career. The redefining process will help you let go of barriers to success and help you take your leadership in a new direction. As part of this metamorphosis, you will need to clarify the purpose and strategic direction of your organization or department, encourage and integrate feedback from followers, and create a diverse environment where employees feel a valued part of the organization.

Your investment in authentic leadership is an investment in the long term—for yourself, for your followers, and for the organization and those it serves. Research has demonstrated the positive effect of authentic leadership on a variety of employee outcomes,[26] including the fact employees have better relationships with organizations when they are inspired by leaders they view as authentic, ethical, balanced, fair, and transparent. In your career as an authentic leader, you will create a pool of well-developed and confident employees who can take the skills and positive experiences they acquired under your leadership into new situations and, in turn, serve others with passion. It all starts with your authentic leadership in the workplace.

Becoming Self-Aware and Exploring Internal Moral Perspectives

There are five components of authentic leadership that a leader's understanding of their inner motivations and guiding moral perspectives: purpose and passion, values and behavior, relationships and connectedness, self-discipline and consistency, and heart and compassion (see Figure 3). These factors are crucial to your evolving career path and your ability to motivate and inspire others.

Purpose and Passion

Authentic leaders derive their specific purpose and direction from the internal motivation—their passion—driving them forward. Followers view authentic leaders as passionate and genuinely caring about their work.

Figure 3

Authentic Leadership Characteristics

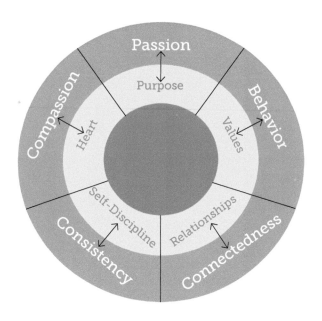

Seeking authentic leadership will help align your internal self with the correct field for your career. To become an authentic leader, you must become deeply aware of your values, beliefs, emotions, self-identity, and talents; in this way, you can stay true to your purpose.[27]

Self-Reflection: *Ask yourself*

What do I care about?

How do I plan to make an impact through my work?

What is my professional purpose?

Values and Behavior

Authentic leaders engage with others through a set of self-established values. They have a clear vision of who they are, where they are going, and how they will get there,[28] so they do not conform to others' views.[29] The result is a leader whose leadership decisions reflect their strong values. In this sense, authentic leadership equates to good leadership because leaders who make decisions that align with genuine values tend to act on behalf of their passions instead of themselves. Conversely, leaders who only make self-serving decisions may be effective decision makers or task managers, but they do not serve others in their leadership roles.

Self-Reflection: *Ask yourself*

What values are part of my foundation?

What behaviors align with my passion?

What is my vision for the future as an authentic leader?

It may be helpful for you to make a list of all the values you care about and rank them in order of importance. Think about these values in the context of leadership. For example, if you rate family as a core value, how is that demonstrated in the workplace? As a leader, do you understand the family responsibilities of the people you manage? Are your company policies family-friendly? Do you know the names of your employees' spouses and children? Do you ask about them? If your behavior as a leader does not align with your core values, explore how to incorporate them. Misalignment is a key indicator that you have not reached your authentic self.

Relationships and Connectedness

Authentic leaders develop strong relationships with others by sharing their own stories and listening to those of others.[30] They open themselves up to others by sharing their thoughts, motives, and vision related to their goals.

This kind of transparency generates trust, loyalty, and commitment in followers. Striving to build such relationships results in deep connections based on trust, respect, and a feeling of mutual obligation.[31]

Self-Discipline and Consistency

Authentic leaders focus on meeting their personal and professional goals. They often display a high energy level and feel compelled to carry out their work in alignment with their values. Often, these leaders set high standards of excellence and have the self-discipline to meet their goals. Followers view these leaders as cool, calm, and consistent, even in challenging situations. Others find security in the predictability and self-directedness of this type of leader.[32]

Heart and Compassion

Authentic leaders have a heart for the work in which they have invested themselves and their careers. Compassion goes hand-in-hand with empathy. *Empathy* refers to the ability to feel what another person feels. *Compassion* refers to the desire to relieve another's suffering or help them in some way. Once you have developed empathy, you can demonstrate compassion. Compassionate leaders empathize with others and offer genuine extensions of help.[33] Acts of compassion create a full circle because they bring leaders more in tune with their authentic selves.[34] Leaders can develop empathy and compassion by listening to others' stories, increasing connectedness, and involving themselves with a variety of people and community projects.[35]

Self-Reflection: *Ask yourself*

How have I used compassion as a leadership tool to benefit myself?

How have I used compassion as a leadership tool to benefit others?

Choosing a Mentor

Many of us learn to lead by following the example set by another, but it isn't enough to adopt the style of a superior just because you desire their power or position. If the shoe doesn't fit, wearing it will hurt. Authentic leadership, on the other hand, makes you effortlessly powerful. This doesn't mean you shouldn't follow the example of others. It just means you should be selective when choosing who to emulate.

Mentors are critical to developing up-and-coming leaders. I have had the privilege to learn from several fabulous mentors in my career. A mentor is a person you have a strong connection with at some level. You may also only work with a mentor for a certain part of your career, and that's okay. In fact, it's normal. No one mentor can be all things to your development. Certain qualities or abilities may have drawn you to this mentor. When that happens, learn all you can from them; seek their wisdom and advice, but don't be afraid to move on or seek guidance elsewhere as your needs and interests grow.

To find a mentor, seek out leaders who inspire you, whether you already work with them (or know them) or not. Observe their leadership choices and give some thought to what you find. Try to pin down what about their style resonates with you. See if you can define their leadership strategies. Once you have some ideas, try them out. See how it feels to adopt one or two. Give it time, and see if your choices or actions feel natural or forced. Also, see what you notice about the people around you as you experiment. How do they respond? Your feelings about these experiments and the responses of your followers will help you find the right mentor for your journey.

Self-Reflection: *Ask yourself*

Have I known any authentic leaders in my life?

What made them authentic?

What do I admire most about them?

Which of their leadership strategies could I use?

Developing a Step-by-Step Plan to Achieve Authentic Leadership

The traits and values of an authentic leader serve as the foundation for their inherent and distinctive leadership style, but authentic leaders are also malleable and accept change as a constant. The style and purpose of authentic leaders culminate from every interaction, sensation, and life experience, whether positive or negative. To remain open to change, you must constantly incorporate what you learn from your real-world experiences into your understanding of your unique passions and authentic styles. Incorporating your defining experiences will directly affect how you receive and perceive new information. You can use your passions to guide your cognitive processing; we all decide how we engage with and draw power from the outside world. As an authentic leader, your passions will be grounded in your values and serve as your standard for behavior and expectations.

After carefully exploring and analyzing questions about your values, passions, past experiences, lessons learned, and ways of responding to personal challenges and workplace situations, it is time to take those responses and craft a path forward. Planning and identifying your goals will take time and effort. Like most things in life, a plan will serve as a guide while also helping you determine where you are in your journey to authentic leadership. Take these seven steps to guide your growth and career development.

Step 1: Decide What Matters to You

Examine and reflect on what is important to you. Your thoughts and reflections from earlier chapters will help to inform this step. Review your answers to previous questions to help you pin down your motives for leadership and clarify your career path.

Self-Reflection: *Ask yourself*

Can I identify a particular field of interest (i.e., health care, business, education, criminal justice) that can guide my career choices?

What role would I like to play in my career (i.e., advocate, executive, expert)?

Step 2: Define Your Values

You've already done some work to identify your personal values, feelings, and beliefs. Now acknowledge and evaluate them as they relate to leadership and your career.

Self-Reflection: *Ask yourself*

Do my values, feelings, and beliefs align with my leadership motives?

Have I identified biases or prejudices that I need to address?

Do I hold religious beliefs that might influence my work choices?

Have I discovered values, feelings, or beliefs that could enhance or limit my career options?

Step 3: Imagine Your Ideal Job
Try to imagine what your ideal job or career would look like by identifying what kind of work will allow you to lead authentically. Begin with fields that align with your authentic self and describe your ideal career in as much detail as possible.

Self-Reflection: *Ask yourself*

What would my typical day look like?

Who or what would I be working with?

Am I suited to lead a group, or should I work alone?

What are my ideal working hours and environment?

What kind of organizational mission most appeals to me?

Step 4: Tell Your Story of Authentic Leadership
To summarize your story of authentic leadership, you'll need to identify
what work and life experiences have shaped your leadership style. Think
of this as telling the story of how you've developed your passion or career
path—much as I told mine in this book's introduction.

Self-Reflection: *Ask yourself*

When did I know I wanted to be an authentic leader?

How have my past experiences shaped my career path?

What experiences have defined my approach to leadership?

How can I connect my past life experiences to my passion and my
desired work environment or career? In other words: What is my story?

Step 5: Define Your Career Goals
To define your career goals, you'll need to have first determined what
kind of career or job best fits your authentic self. Sometimes big or far-
reaching goals can feel too distant or difficult, which can leave you feeling
unmotivated or defeated. Avoid these pitfalls and keep yourself moving

forward by breaking your goals into smaller, more manageable parts. Elaborate on all of your goals, even if you're not exactly sure where or how they all fit together right now.

What is a reasonable 3-year goal?

What do I hope to achieve in the next 5-years?

What can I accomplish by the 7-year mark?

Where do I want my career to be in 10 years?

Step 6: Identify Ways to Grow

Determine which areas of work and leadership challenge you. Then adopt a mindset that casts these areas of needed growth not as weaknesses but as opportunities for practice. These are your opportunities to make yourself a better and more authentic leader. Make a plan for developing yourself by pursuing opportunities that require you to improve in the areas where you need practice or development. For example, if the career path you desire will require public speaking and you do not feel comfortable speaking in front of groups, you might start by presenting to your family, then to a social or church group. When you are ready, seek out work opportunities to speak publicly to develop your skills in a professional setting. You may also identify areas for improvement as leading meetings or coaching others. Start in your comfort zone; perfect your skills, and move to the next opportunity to continue your growth. As you go, measure your progress against the skills needed in your desired career.

Step 7: Network

It's finally time to begin your search for this career or job! Although traditional job searches (using headhunters, online jobs forums, or other

What are my strengths? In what areas could I do better?

How can I improve in my areas of needed growth?

Are there any social, volunteer, or work opportunities that could help me develop my areas of needed growth?

Am I ready to pursue this career now, or do I still have work to do?

What barriers or obstacles must I overcome before I can pursue my new career path or desired position?

What is my plan for overcoming the barriers I face?

job advertisements) are useful, networking is the most effective way to switch careers or find new employment.[36] Consequently, you will need to find ways to meet people and network with those already established in the field. Once you have identified people of interest, you can approach them directly or through a professional organization. In your initial contact, explain how you learned about the individual, describe your career interests, and then ask if they would be willing to meet with you to share their expertise. Of course, it's always useful to also look for job postings using associations or other organizations that support your field of interest. You might find a job posting where you want to submit an application, but scanning these kinds of advertisements will also inform you of what kinds of positions are available in your field, what skills employers are seeking, and what language they use to describe that work.

As you move through these seven steps, remember that authentic leaders are malleable and accept change as a constant. Also, understand that your career goals or development plan may evolve over time. This could require you to circle back through these steps to make adjustments. Remember to intentionally plan to develop yourself at all levels and hold others to similarly high expectations while giving praise often.

Self-Reflection: *Ask yourself*

Who do I know with experience in or knowledge of this field?

How can I reach out and connect with these people?

How can I meet others in my desired field?

Is there an association or other professional organization I can join?

Finally, you must be willing to seek feedback from others while allowing time to analyze your own journey. It is okay to define what you want to achieve. In fact, the more clearly you can articulate your goals and develop a timeline, the more likely you are to realize your aspirations. Treat your plan as a work in progress by reevaluating it every 6 months to a year. This could also mean dreaming a new dream or developing new goals along the way. All of this is part of the growth process that will lead you to the career path that will best propel you on your journey to being the authentic leader you aspire to be.

Identifying values
What do you care about?

_____

_____

_____

How do you plan to make an impact through your work?

_____

_____

_____

What is your professional purpose?

_____

_____

_____

Comparing values and behavior
What values are part of your foundation?

_____

_____

_____

What behaviors align with your passion?

_____

_____

_____

What is your vision for the future as an authentic leader?

_____

_____

_____

Relationships and connectedness

Do you make an effort to listen to others? Provide examples.

_____

_____

_____

Have you cultivated trust, loyalty, and commitment from others? Who? How?

_____

_____

_____

Which of your relationships could use more work to develop trust and loyalty?

_____

_____

_____

Assessing self-discipline and consistency
Do you maintain energy levels for high-impact situations? How? When?

_____

_____

_____

Are there situations where you could have been more consistent?

_____

_____

_____

In what ways do you seek excellence?

_____

_____

_____

Developing compassion
How have you used compassion as a leadership tool to benefit yourself?

_____

_____

_____

How have you used compassion as a leadership tool to benefit others?

_____

_____

_____

Choosing a mentor
Have you known any authentic leaders in your life?

_____

_____

_____

What made them authentic?

_____

_____

_____

What do you admire most about them?

_____

_____

_____

Which of their leadership strategies could you use?

_____

_____

_____

Develop a Step-by-Step Plan

Personal priorities

Can you identify a particular field of interest (i.e., health care, business, education, criminal justice) that can guide your career choices?

_____

_____

_____

What role would you like to play in your career (i.e., advocate, executive, expert)?

_____

_____

_____

Values

Do your values, feelings, and beliefs align with your leadership motives?

_____

_____

_____

Have you identified biases or prejudices that you need to address?

_____

_____

_____

Do you hold religious beliefs that might influence your work choices?

_____

_____

_____

Have you discovered values, feelings, or beliefs that could enhance or limit your career options?

_____

_____

_____

Your ideal job
What would your typical day look like?

_____

_____

_____

Who or what would you be working with?

_____

_____

_____

Are you suited to lead a group, or should you work alone?

_____

_____

What are your ideal working hours and environment?

_____

_____

_____

What kind of organizational mission most appeals to you?

_____

_____

_____

Telling your story
When did you know you wanted to be an authentic leader?

_____

_____

_____

How have your past experiences shaped your career path?

_____

_____

_____

What experiences have defined your approach to leadership?

_____

_____

_____

How can you connect your past life experiences to your passion and your desired work environment or career? In other words: What is your story?

_____

_____

_____

Setting career goals
What is a reasonable 3-year goal?

_____

_____

_____

What do you hope to achieve in the next 5-years?

_____

_____

_____

What can you accomplish by the 7-year mark?

_____

_____

_____

Where do you want your career to be in 10 years?

_____

_____

_____

Areas of needed growth
What are your strengths? In what areas could you do better?

_____

_____

_____

How can you improve in your areas of needed growth?

_____

_____

_____

Are there any social, volunteer, or work opportunities that could help you develop your areas of needed growth?

_____

_____

_____

Are you ready to pursue this career now, or do you still have work to do?

_____

_____

_____

What barriers or obstacles must you overcome before you can pursue your new career path or desired position?

_____

_____

_____

What is your plan for overcoming the barriers you face?

_____

_____

_____

Networking
Who do you know with experience in or knowledge of this field?

_____

_____

_____

How can you reach out and connect with these people?

_____

_____

_____

How can you meet others in your desired field?

_____

_____

_____

Is there an association or other professional organization you can join?

_____

_____

_____

Chapter 5:
Adding Value to Your Organization

Leadership has been shown to be the most critical means of developing organizational culture.[37] A leader's influence on organizational culture, willingness to embrace change, and ability to meet established goals makes them integral to an organization's success. Also, today's rapidly diversifying workforce requires the authentic leader's unique ability to listen and build relationships. It has been shown that this ability, along with the other skills of authentic leadership, can significantly affect organizational factors such as performance, culture, employee empowerment, trust in management, commitment, emotional intelligence, and learning.[38,39] These factors combine to have a direct positive effect on an organization.[40] A growing understanding of authentic leadership and its importance to organizational success is changing how leaders interact with and manage employees.[41]

Creating Positive Organizational Cultures
Inspiring Others
Authentic leaders have become self-aware, morally in tune, transparent, and balanced in their work and life. Consequently, they can follow their strong moral compass and build mutually respectful relationships that can motivate and empower a diverse group of individuals. By inspiring employees to perform at peak levels, authentic leaders can increase an organization's efficiency, effectiveness, and productivity.[42] Key traits associated with authentic leaders include confidence, hopefulness, optimism, and a high level of ethical mindfulness. Employees led by authentic leaders are likely to be more creative, have improved self-confidence, and demonstrate overall high performance in the organization.[43]

How have I inspired others through my leadership?

What do I do to create inspiring situations?

What steps have I taken to develop the skills of others?

What steps have I taken to help others reach their aspirations?

How have I used the goals and passions of others to create change?

Building Trust

Authentic leaders interact positively with followers. These positive interactions establish an environment of trust where employees feel valued, which in turn makes them willing to engage more deeply in their daily work. When leaders establish trust, employees buy into change more easily, increasing productivity. Authentic leaders positively influence organizations by developing trust, engagement, well-being, and performance. In fact, managers who develop authentic leadership skills have been shown to decrease negative workplace behaviors such as stealing, damaging property, and reducing work time through late arrivals and long breaks.[44]

Authentic leaders can build trust by acting as role models. This can involve modeling the following desired behaviors:

- Listen to employees and make them feel heard
- Be transparent by explaining and sharing the common goals
- Take responsibility, even if the outcomes are unexpected
- Trust your followers as trust goes both ways in a relationship
- Coach employees rather than command their work
- Support collaboration and encourage teamwork

Your followers will trust you if your actions demonstrate an intention to help them grow and develop in their careers. To contribute to your followers' growth, make an effort to delegate responsibilities. This will show you have confidence in them and give them opportunities to develop skills and gain experience. Expand these efforts by collaborating with others to find opportunities for peers and followers to grow, and take time to identify those individuals with leadership potential and mentor them on their path.

It is also important to establish performance metrics that align with elements of authentic leadership. If followers know what is expected of them and understand how to measure their progress in meeting those expectations, they will trust you and invest in the job at hand. Also, aligning performance metrics with qualities of authentic leadership will encourage your followers to act in authentic ways. Some elements of authentic leadership you can incorporate into performance metrics include transparency, a moral perspective, balanced processing, and self-awareness.[45]

Each of these leadership components comes with associated actions or behaviors. Those associated with transparency and having a moral perspective include: saying what you mean, admitting mistakes, speaking your mind, telling the truth, staying in tune with your emotions and feelings, turning beliefs into actions, and making decisions and taking positions based on grounded values and ethics. To practice balanced processing, you must be willing to challenge a particular position, analyze data, and listen to various viewpoints.

Behaviors associated with self-awareness might include giving and receiving feedback, embracing others' capabilities, reevaluating your position based on all the information, and seeking action that will have an impact. By adopting these actions yourself, you will model authentic leadership for your followers, and including these elements in performance metrics will allow you to use performance reviews to encourage all members of your team to adopt authentic behaviors that will serve themselves, the team, and the organization.

Communicating openly

Authentic leaders must develop an organizational culture that is honest, trusting, and empowering to all followers. An essential element of organizational leadership is effective communication. Leaders' communication affects employee experiences daily.[46] As an authentic leader, you should communicate openly with employees and encourage them to share ideas and concerns. In one study, authentic leadership fostered internal communication and a positive organizational culture that was found to be more supportive, reward-focused, and stable. The study also showed a substantial correlation between leadership communication and employees' input before leaders made decisions. There was also a link between openness, participation, and empowerment.[47] A researcher noted communication shapes culture and employee interactions. This means authentic leadership and organizational culture are mutually influential.[48]

One strategy for instilling and maintaining open communication is to hold what I call a SMART meeting. The SMART acronym is used in other fields for goal setting, but I have adapted it here to stand for simple, mindful, authentic, realistic, and transparent. When meeting with your team, holding one-on-one conferences, or conducting coaching and mentoring sessions, remember the following:

- Keep things *simple*.
- Be *mindful* and present.
- Be *authentic* in your actions.
- Set *realistic* expectations.
- Be *transparent* about thoughts and goals.

For example, if holding a meeting on new procedures, don't get bogged down dictating every little step. Focus on the topic at hand and keep the meeting simple by gently guiding the conversation so it doesn't drift from topic to topic. To remain mindful, avoid getting distracted by past mistakes or letting the meeting drag on. These missteps can lead to boredom and frustration. Being mindful and present will also help you give the topic your full attention rather than rushing through because you feel pressured to address other tasks. This kind of focus will help you move meetings forward and will encourage others to come to your meetings prepared. To be authentic, share your honest thoughts and ideas while allowing others to share theirs—and take care to listen when they do! When wrapping up, revisit the meeting objectives to be sure you've addressed them. Then set realistic next steps so you don't overload the group. Be transparent by clearly sharing the overall goals of the project, meeting, or topic to ensure everyone understands what they are working toward and why.

Behaving Ethically

Employee retention, positive outcomes, and efforts to attract new talent rely on ethical standards. Authentic leaders show appreciation and respect for employees while building a positive company culture. Ethical practice received a lot of media attention after a variety of unethical leadership events caused large organizations to fail. Several organizations experienced collapse due to unethical business practices. Enron collapsed after claiming fake holdings and using off-the-books accounting practices. HealthSouth exaggerated company profits to woo investors. Royal Dutch Shell inflated its oil reserves figures. Adelphia inflated revenues and earnings to gain additional investors, and Marsh McLennan committed mutual fund fraud. Leaders in these cases did not make decisions rooted in the kinds of values and ethics that define authentic leadership. Instead, they succumbed to pressure, temptation, and other corporate forces that led them to falsify or make up information to help their organization remain in business. In most cases, unethical leaders respond to financial incentives that keep them engaged in dishonest practices. As an authentic leader, you will avoid these types of downfalls because you will have learned the value of providing employees a positive work environment and conducting business in an ethical and socially acceptable manner. [49]

Authentic leaders value ethical behavior and contribute to the existence of an ethical culture at their organizations. The more transparent a leader can be, the more trust they develop. Consequently, ethical boundaries become clear and valued. *Workplace deviance*—stealing, damaging company property, arriving late to work, taking extra breaks, and not following directions from supervisors—leads to high organizational costs. These include reduced productivity, negative work climates, and damaged organizational reputations. Deviant attitudes and behaviors can significantly affect job satisfaction, turnover, and job performance,[50] so it is important for you to develop high-quality relationships with subordinates

64

who feel supported and trusted through open communication and ongoing feedback.[51]

Empowering and Engaging Followers

Authentic leaders enhance organizational culture by purposefully engaging employees. To engage your followers, begin by giving them freedom and flexibility in their work while also offering room for growth and development. Allow for employees to use their strengths and abilities to positively impact their workplace environment and work outcomes.

Shared Reflection

Change can be challenging on any level, but change can also be an energetic force that evolves processes and workflows to better serve the customer. No matter the field of work, we all strive to serve our customers to the best of our abilities. In health care, front-line staff have the greatest level of interaction with clients and thus have the greatest ability to meet customer needs. Because of this interaction, front-line staff also have the best ideas.

In one facility where I worked, staff were encouraged to share ideas for change and to lead the change initiatives. Employees shared ideas for change on a giant whiteboard at annual meetings. The group then reached a consensus on which projects would move forward. Front-line staff led the change initiatives while management supported the efforts by creating policy and process. No matter their role or tenure, any staff member could select an initiative they felt compelled to support.

The outcomes were amazing! The front-line staff felt engaged and empowered to make improvements for those they served, and the residents we cared for benefited from the results. Many of the projects had quality-of-life implications for residents and helped boost our satisfaction surveys from residents, families, and facility employees.

Authentic leaders can also engage followers by helping them establish individual goals and ways of measuring their progress.[52] A vital element of the authentic leader–follower relationship is the leader's ability to help develop the follower. Followers who are engaged in facility projects and empowered to implement their own ideas grow personally and professionally. Organizations benefit when leaders develop employees this way because employees feel invested in the attainment of organizational goals.[53]

Strategies for Developing Teams

An authentic leader must cultivate strategic relationships to lead an effective team. Groups led by authentic leaders have better group cohesion and teamwork; this can be attributed to certain patterns of behavior, including inspiring and promoting followers while fostering a positive ethical climate.[54] These factors especially pertain to service-related professions dealing directly with people's lives. Developing teams involves a complex set of skills and activities.

To be an effective team member and leader, you must develop your team by establishing strategic goals, building upon you team's strengths, identifying skill gaps, and addressing opportunities for team growth. You must also evaluate the team's ability to shift and support a variety of goals. This involves identifying external supports and recognizing when the need for new positions arises. Your evaluation of team functioning may also involve looking beyond the immediate team to form collaborative partnerships with ad-hoc teams. Do not be afraid to think outside the box. As a flexible and transparent authentic leader, you may skip hierarchy levels and network by capitalizing on team members' individual strengths and interests.

Authentic leaders can more easily facilitate collaboration in and out of the team if they personally know each team member well enough to foster development and connections among team members. As an authentic leader, work to cultivate one-on-one relationships. You can also share ideas in a two-way format by asking for feedback as a leader from your follower. This means you must be able to shift your mindset from the big picture to provide individuals with limited updates, conduct individual goal check-ins, and review individual strengths. You must also incorporate support for innovation, creativity, and individual development.

The cultivation of authentic teams will have lasting effects with innumerable benefits. You will establish your legacy as an authentic leader who helped others develop. You will build effective, empowered, and authentic leaders and followers at each level in your organization who will impact the organization's overall operations and its employees for many years to come. You will create effective and dynamic teams that support and retain front-line staff. You will support and sustain career progress and

Self-Reflection: *Ask yourself*

Do I know my team members?

Who has what strength or talent?

Who works well together?

What are the commonalities on which I can build?

What deficits must I solve to build or strengthen my team?

How can I develop effective and empowered leaders using the authentic skills and talents of my team members?

Do I know how my team members want to grow their careers?

What are the passions, motivations, and abilities of each of my team members? How do their stories influence these passions?

succession planning efforts, and you will produce engaged and fulfilled team members who care about the work they do.

Leading Organizational Change

Implementing organizational change is no easy task. It takes authentic leaders equipped to help followers prepare for the change, accept the change, and then follow through with the new processes. In a 2017 study, Haroon, Bakari, and colleagues found that leaders are central to the success of organizational change.[55] This is not surprising, because leaders have so much influence over followers' ability to meet or exceed organizational goals.[56] When an organization sets a goal to achieve change, an authentic leader is needed to bring that goal to fruition.

Authentic leaders help connect employees to organizational goals and to the changes that must occur to reach those goals. I have seen authentic leaders in action, sharing goals, developing plans for change, and working alongside followers to help them achieve the desired outcomes.

Authentic leaders conduct themselves in such a manner that their actions and words fundamentally align, even during times of significant change. The uniform consistency of the leader's words and behaviors builds trust

Shared Reflection

Conducting surveys in the long-term care industry can be quite intense; survey outcomes can mean financial penalities and might affect a facility's ability to remain open for business. An impending survey generated considerable stress and fear among employees at a facility where I worked. To improve perceptions of the survey, the facility leader treated the survey as a way to adopt a mindset of continuous improvement. With this approach, the leader embedded the idea of survey preparation into the everyday work environment. The leader shared this view, presenting it as a goal so all team members could understand how they could contribute toward this goal by simply doing their daily work. This meant all team members—leaders and followers—participated in the process. By changing the approach and communicating it effectively, this leader changed the work culture and shifted the view of the survey from one of fear to one of benchmarking and goal setting. Oftentimes, it takes the authenticity of the leader to show followers that change is OK, and in many cases, the outcomes represent improvements.

and commitment between the organization and its employees. This relationship also helps drive the change process. Employees hold their organizations in higher regard when they see their leaders as trustworthy and credible. Change also occurs more easily when followers see their leader as acting authentically. The authentic leader further cultivates relationships with followers during times of change by practicing transparency and maintaining open two-way communication. These actions keep employees engaged, developing a positive work environment that shapes employee opinion of the organization.[57]

Characteristics That Effect Organizational Change

Other factors influence organizational performance and authentic leadership. Strong links appear to exist among the authentic leader, the response from their followers, and organizational performance.[58] The attributes of self-efficacy, hope, optimism, and resilience are fundamental to an authentic leader's ability to inspire and motivate followers in ways that benefit overall organizational performance.

Self-Efficacy

Authentic leaders have a high level of self-efficacy and can help others develop this skill. *Self-efficacy* refers to a person's belief in their ability to accomplish goals (i.e., confidence). Confident leaders and followers are more likely to endure, stay the course, and persist, even when things do not go as planned.[59] These leaders welcome the challenge to reach their goals and continually move forward. They also help followers gain skills to further develop in this area. Self-efficacy also contributes to excellent work performance and the self-confidence needed for leaders and their followers to succeed under the pressure of a new challenge.[60]

Hope

Authentic leaders use hope to inspire followers and build trust.[61,62] Hope is a state of mind most often related to a specific event that helps individuals work with a plan toward a goal. Hope can be considered a combination of the will and the way to goal achievement. Using open communication to create hope among followers can empower them to set goals and decide a course to reach them. When leaders and followers feel hopeful, they can increase organizational profits, employee satisfaction, and retention.[63] As an authentic leader, you will need hope to set goals and have the will to stay the course until they meet them.

Optimism

Optimism grows from a perspective on life that is positive, ethical, and inclined toward reaching set goals.[64] *Optimism* refers to the positive expectations an individual holds about an outcome. Authentic leaders must practice optimism while inspiring it in their followers. Doing so can create happiness, pride, satisfaction, and enthusiasm.[65] To accomplish this, leaders can recognize past successes and use them to fuel optimism about the next challenge. Followers who receive praise and view their leader as capable and optimistic will follow their lead.

Resilience

Resilience refers to the ability of an authentic leader to use unforeseen circumstances as a springboard for recovering from and adjusting to a situation.[66] Authentic leaders absorb hardships, utilizing experiences and resources to recover quickly and ultimately emerge as a better version of themselves.[67] This further develops authenticity and benefits followers who see their leader modeling resilience. For example, resilience becomes important when a project proceeds differently than planned, requiring a new plan to keep the project on track. Resilient leaders anticipate that all is not lost when their first plan fails because they understand the path to the desired outcome has simply changed. They see and accept a less-than-perfect situation as a work in progress.

Figure 4 illustrates the progression you will take on your journey to becoming an organizational authentic leader. The journey begins internally. Once you have grounded yourself through internal work, you will advance to outside work where you will examine how your actions and leadership decisions affect those around you. Your development culminates with the impacts you have on the organizational culture.

Figure 4

Progression to Organizational Authentic Leader

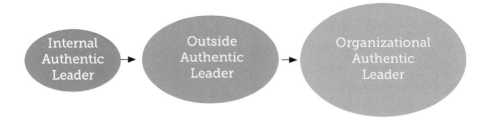

Inspiring others

How have you inspired others through your leadership?

_____

_____

_____

What do you do to create inspiring situations?

_____

_____

_____

What steps have you taken to develop the skills of others?

_____

_____

_____

What steps have you taken to help others reach their aspirations?

_____

_____

_____

How have you used the goals and passions of others to create change?

_____

_____

Developing relationships

Do you know your team members?

_____

_____

_____

Who has what strength or talent?

_____

_____

_____

Who works well together?

_____

_____

_____

What are the commonalities on which you can build?

_____

_____

_____

What deficits must you solve to build or strengthen your team?

_____

_____

_____

How can you develop effective and empowered leaders using the authentic skills and talents of your team members?

_____

_____

_____

Do you know how your team members want to grow their careers?

_____

_____

_____

What are the passions, motivations, and abilities of each of your team members? How do their stories influence these passions?

_____

_____

_____

Chapter 6:
Authentic Leadership in Action

As a leader, you can use your authenticity to cultivate the respect, trust, and credibility you desire. When your followers perceive you as a genuine person who is also a leader, you will have achieved the defining step in winning the hearts and minds of followers and those served by your organization. To be an authentic leader, you must overcome any sense of fear related to sharing too much of your inner self. To ascend the highest levels of leadership excellence, you must overcome that fear and be yourself when engaging with people. Developing authenticity requires reflecting on what this kind of leadership means in practical terms and how others view authentic qualities in leadership. Authentic leaders possess unique qualities that make their thoughts, words, and deeds truly authentic. There are several ways you can continue the process of developing into an authentic leader.

Invest Time and Effort to Truly Understand Your Values
In leadership, your values serve as your compass; they will show you the way when you feel lost or are struggling for answers. Yet, you first must clearly know your values. Ensure you understand what matters to you and base your approach to leadership on those things. Never sacrifice your values because they are the source of your authentic approach. If you become confused about your values, or if you sacrifice them, you can appear shallow and superficial to those you lead. Authentic leaders who value individuals, honest effort, and humility will shine for others to follow. If you lead from your values, those searching for a beacon will look to you and follow.

Lead From Your Heart; Implement With Your Head
Once you understand your values and principles, you can then identify your passion. Colleagues and followers like to see passion and heart because they see a cause worth fighting for, which inspires them to join the fight. Sterile or robotic leadership will not help you win the hearts and minds of others. Neither, however, will unconsidered decisions, so while leading with your heart, implement with your brain. You must combine

passion and structure to accomplish your goals. Managing responses to setbacks takes both rational thought and emotional intelligence. For example, let's say you are implementing a new service you feel passionate about. After putting much blood, sweat, and tears into it, you discover you lack the funding to immediately move the entire project forward. Does this setback mean all is lost? The heart wants the project fully implemented now because the benefits to those served shouldn't wait, but the brain understands this project will take time and money. Instead of letting emotions control the outcome, the brain must step in and find a different path toward the goal. The brain can solve the problem, realizing that the project can be completed, but only if broken down into steps and budgeted over time. The heart and the brain make a very powerful and effective combination when used in the right balance.

Work Toward Excellence, Not Perfection

As authentic leaders, when we show our heart, the appropriate actions follow. However, despite our best efforts, all leaders make mistakes. Authentic leadership includes taking responsibility for errors. Nobody expects you to be perfect. In fact, the leader who professes to be perfect loses credibility and authenticity. Followers expect and will appreciate when you admit and embrace your mistakes, then work hard to move forward in your mission. Mistakes won't define you, but how you respond to them will. If you respond with honesty and integrity, your colleagues will rally around you and continue the effort to achieve excellence—not perfection.

Think With Sincerity

The process of thinking serves to connect your values and your actions: How you think translates values into behavior. You must start from your values and then make decisions without pretense. This way, your actions will be defined by genuine intent based upon an empathic approach to leadership. You are what you think, and colleagues can see that every minute of the day. Authentic thinking starts from a simple premise: that you genuinely seek win-win outcomes without manipulating situations for self-gain. If you approach situations with a growth mindset and the belief that a team characterized by mutual trust and support can share challenges, you will enhance outcomes. People see authentic leaders as individuals who want to help others achieve desired results. Followers will reward your sincere actions with long-term loyalty and engagement.

Behave Ethically and With Integrity at All Times

The authentic leader should always be mindful that people see actions before they hear words. Consequently, you must act in a way that demonstrates your commitment to your values. Making the right calls instead of the easy ones will solidify the perception that you are committed to doing what is right. Colleagues recognize authenticity in transparency and consistency of action. It is important for authentic leaders to do the right thing, even when nobody is watching. If you commit to this ideal, you will demonstrate authenticity in thought and deed and inspire those around you to do the same.

Encourage Honest Action Through Honest Communication

You can think and act with honest values and intentions at your core, but what comes out of your mouth will play a crucial role in how others perceive your actions. Honesty in communication means you explain what you know and admit what you do not know. Nobody expects leaders to have all the answers, but they do expect leaders to admit they do *not* have all the answers and work tirelessly to find solutions. Whether you have an answer or not, you must practice humility by seeking the input of others and recognizing their contributions, being modest and measured, and providing dignified responses to provocation. Your words can only contribute to your authenticity when they align with your behaviors. Don't be a leader whose message is, in effect, "Do as I say, not as I do." Rather, operate under the premise, "Follow my lead."

Be Optimistic

Overly ideological views create the impression of too much theory and not enough reality. Yet, we all need dreams to which we can aspire. You can set high goals—reach for your dreams!—but be sensible and realistic in your approach. This will show your flexibility and inspire confidence. Progress is rarely linear, so be prepared to make adaptations that demonstrates that you accept that fact. The vision of where you want to go, however, is the light that must be shined for others to follow. You must stay positive as you pursue that vision, and do so with visible energy. As an authentic leader, you cannot play the absentee landlord; you must engage in the moment with your team. If you don't show that you appreciate their challenges, you'll risk appearing out of touch. Adopt a mindset of realistic optimism.

Find Work–Life Balance

Followers appreciate a leader who talks openly about the balance among work, family, and friends. They do not want to be led by someone with a one-dimensional view of life, but rather someone who understands and empathizes with the complexities of life. You can also demonstrate you value work–life balance by approaching decisions flexibly and using the emotional intelligence discussed in Chapter 2 as needed. Although rules matter, so do people's individual circumstances. Use balance and sincerity to accommodate individual needs while maintaining group or organizational objectives. As an authentic leader, you can model this balance in your approach to professional and personal needs.

Build a Legacy Through Authentic Leadership

By building a legacy as an authentic leader, you will garner significant respect; you will show awareness of broader responsibilities and your balanced perception of what success means. As an authentic leader and decision maker, you can become an example of balance, maturity, and responsibility. Followers will see you as someone who is unwilling to settle for short-term benefits at the expense of letting seeds grow for long-term gain. If you consider legacy a fundamental goal, you will need to show colleagues your authentic approach.

Remember, achieving authenticity does not require a set of conditions associated with age, seniority, or experience. However, it does require you to invest heavily in understanding and committing to your values so those values can inform your thoughts, actions, and communications. By practicing fearlessly authentic leadership, you will deeply inspire others and set a positive example for peers and followers alike.

Conclusion

Authentic leadership is dynamic because it starts and ends with the individual leader's core values. Consequently, developing authenticity begins with your own strong values, ethics, and morals. You will embark on your journey by raising your self-awareness and understanding your moral perspectives. Then you must open yourself to hearing others' views and work to improve your communication skills to be sure you are always transparent and honest. As your journey to authenticity continues, you must develop attributes of confidence, hope, optimism, and resilience to overcome the challenges you will encounter along the way. Authentic leaders must articulate their purpose and passion; know their values and how they impact their behavior; and work to develop relationships with peers, followers, and those they serve. These leaders display self-discipline and consistency while also showing heart and compassion for their daily work.

Just by reading this book, you've come so far! As you continue on your leadership journey to step into the authentic you, remember these steps.

1. Embrace your true, best self.
2. Define who you want to be as a leader and what feels right.
3. Discover your strengths and step into them.
4. Learn about your blind spots and address them.
5. Find an appropriate mentor or those with similar passions.
6. Create your own professional development plan.

Once you have become an authentic leader, you will be able to use that leadership to positively impact organizational performance and outcomes. Authentic leaders can profoundly influence organizational culture and significantly, positively influence overall organizational performance. As an authentic leader, you will inspire followers, build lasting trust, embrace constant and open communication, display ethical behavior, and empower and engage team members at all levels of the organization—all while leading positive organizational change. But be patient! Authentic leadership takes years to cultivate. Once achieved, however, you can use it to create a deep sense of balance and achievement among your followers while significantly improving organizational performance.

Endnotes

1   James E. Henderson and Wayne K. Hoy, "Leader Authenticity."
2   Sadaf Iqbal et al., "The Impact of Authentic Leadership."
3   Fred Walumbwa et al., "Psychological Processes."
4   Peter Northouse, *Leadership: Theory and Practice.*
5   Ibid.
6   Linjuan Men, "Internal Reputation Management."
7   Ibid.
8   Iqbal et al., "The Impact of Authentic Leadership."
9   Shahid Khan, "Impact of Authentic Leaders on Organizational Performance."
10 Fred Walumbwa et al., "Authentic Leadership: Development and Validation."
11 Northouse, *Leadership.*
12 Samaneh Mohammadpour et al., "Authentic Leadership: A New Approach to Leadership."
13 Kumar Alok, "Authentic Leadership and Psychological Ownership."
14 Margaret Diddams and Glenna C. Chang, "Only Human."
15 Northouse, *Leadership.*
16 Mohammadpour et al., "Authentic Leadership."
17 Iqbal et al., "The Impact of Authentic Leadership."
18 Northouse, *Leadership.*
19 Joanna Furmanczyk, "The Cross-Cultural Leadership Aspect."
20 Lesia Yasinski, "Authentic Leadership."
21 Yasinski, "Authentic Leadership."
22 Men, "Internal Reputation Management."
23 Yasinski, "Authentic Leadership."
24 Ibid.
25 Oleg N. Medvedev et al., "Network Analysis of Mindfulness Facets."
26 Walumbwa et al., "Psychological Processes."
27 Hua Jiang and Linjuan Men, "Creating an Engaged Workforce."
28 Bill George, *Authentic Leadership.*
29 Jiang and Men, "Creating an Engaged Workforce."
30 Northouse, *Leadership.*
31 Ibid.
32 Ibid.
33 Ibid.
34 George, *Authentic Leadership.*
35 Northouse, *Leadership.*
36 Karl D. Majeske and James S. Serocki, "Achieve."
37 Elvira Nica, "Moral Leadership."
38 Derya Kara et al., "The Effects of Leadership Style."
39 Carol Wong and Heather Laschinger, "Authentic Leadership Performance."
40 Mohammadpour et al., "Authentic Leadership."
41 Kara et al., "The Effects of Leadership Style."
42 Mohammadpour et al., "Authentic Leadership."

43   Ibid.
44   Hakan Erkutlu and Jamel Chafra, "Effects of Trust."
45   Biplab Datta, "Assessing the Effectiveness of Authentic Leadership."
46   Linjuan Men and Hua Jiang, "Cultivating Quality Employee-Organization Relationships."
47   Men and Jiang, "Cultivating Quality Employee-Organization Relationships."
48   Bruce Berger, "Read My Lips."
49   Men and Jiang, "Cultivating Quality Employee-Organization Relationships."
50   Erkutlu and Chafra, "Effects of Trust."
51   Ibid.
52   Qaiser Mehmood et al., "Authentic Leadership and Followers' In-Role and Extra-Role Performance."
53   Ibid.
54   Carlos Lopez et al., "Authentic Leadership, Group Cohesion and Group Identification."
55   Haroon Bakari et al., "How Does Authentic Leadership Influence Planned Organizational Change?"
56   Men, "Internal Reputation Management."
57   Ibid.
58   Khan, "Impact of Authentic Leaders on Organization Performance."
59   Northouse, *Leadership*.
60   Ibid.
61   Ibid.
62   Men, "Internal Reputation Management."
63   Khan, "Impact of Authentic Leaders on Organization Performance."
64   Northouse, *Leadership*.
65   Khan, "Impact of Authentic Leaders on Organization Performance."
66   Northouse, *Leadership*.
67   Khan, "Impact of Authentic Leaders on Organization Performance."

References

Alok, K. (2014). Authentic leadership and psychological ownership: Investigation of interrelations. *Leadership & Organizational Development Journal, 35*(4), 266–285. https://doi.org/10.1108/LODJ-06-2012-0080

Bakari, H., Hunjra, A., & Niazi, G. (2017). How does authentic leadership influence planned organizational change? The role of employees' perceptions: integration of theory of planned behavior and Lewin's three-step model. *Journal of Change Management, 17*(2), 155–187. https://doi.org/10.1080/14697017.2017.1299370

Berger, B. (2014). Read my lips: Leaders, supervisors, and culture are the foundations of strategic employee communication. *The Research Journal of Institute for Public Relations.*

Bradberry, T., & Greaves, J. (2009). *Emotional intelligence 2.0.* Talent Smart.

Datta, B. (2015). Assessing the effectiveness of authentic leadership. *International Journal of Leadership Studies, 9*(1).

Diddams, M., & Change, G. C. (2012). Only human: Exploring the nature of weakness in authentic leadership. *The Leadership Quarterly, 23*(3), 593–603. https://doi.org/10.1016/j.leaqua.2011.12.010

Erkutlu, H., & Chafra, J. (2013). Effects of trust and psychological contract violation on authentic leadership and organizational deviance. *Management Research Review, 36*(9), 828–848. https://doi.org/10.1108/MRR-06-2012-0136

Furmanczyk, J. (2010). The cross-cultural leadership aspect. *Journal of Intercultural Management, 2,* 67–82.

George, B. (2003). *Authentic leadership: Rediscovering the secrets to creating lasting value.* San Francisco, CA: Jossey-Bass.

Goleman, D. (2004, January). What makes a leader? IQ and technical skills are important, but emotional intelligence is the sine qua non of leadership. *Harvard Business Review.* https://hbr.org/2004/01/what-makes-a-leader

Henderson, J., & Hoy, W. (1982). *Leader authenticity: The development and test of an operational measure* [Paper presentation]. 66th Annual Meeting of the American Educational Research Association, New York, NY.

Iqbal, S., Farid, T., Ma, J., Khattak, A., & Nurunnabi, M. (2018). The impact of authentic leadership on organizational citizenship behaviors and the mediating role of corporate social responsibility in the banking sector of Pakistan. *The Journal of Sustainability, 10*(2), 1–11. https://doi.org/10.3390/su10072170

Jiang, H., & Men, R. L. (2015). Creating an engaged workforce: The impact of authentic leadership, transparent organizational communication, and work-life enrichment. *Communication Research, (44)*2, 225–243. https://doi.org/10.1177/0093650215613137

Kara, D., Uysal, M., Sirgy, M., & Lee, G. (2013). The effects of leadership style on employee well-being in hospitality. *International Journal of Hospitality Management, 34*(6), 9-18. https://doi.org/10.1016/j.ijhm.2013.02.001

Khan, S. (2010). Impact of authentic leaders on organization performance. *International Journal of Business and Management, 5*(12), 167–172. https://doi.org/10.5539/ijbm.v5n12p167

Lopez, C., Alonso, F., Morales, M., & Leon, J. (2015). Authentic leadership, group cohesion and group identification in security and emergency teams. *Psicothema, 27*(1), 59–64.

Medvedev, O. N., Cervin, M., Barcaccia, B., Siegert, R. J., Roemer, A., & Krageloh, C. U. (2021). Network analysis of mindfulness facets, affect, compassion, and distress. *Mindfulness, 12*, 911–922. https://doi-org.lib-proxy.radford.edu/10.1007/s12671-020-01555-8

Mehmood, Q., Hamstra, M., Nawab, S., & Vriend, T. (2016). Authentic leadership and followers' in-role and extra-role performance: The mediating role of followers' learning goal orientation. *Journal of Occupational and Organizational Psychology, 89*, 877–883. https://doi.org/10.1111/joop.12153

Majeske, K., & Serocki, J. (2009). *Business Education Innovation Journal, 1*(2), 59–67.

Men, L. (2014). Internal reputation management: The impact of authentic leadership and transparent communication. *Corporate Reputation Review, 17*(4), 254–272. https://doi.org/10.1057/crr.2014.14

Men, L., & Jiang, H. (2016). Cultivating quality employee-organization relationships: The interplay among organization leadership, culture, and communication. *International Journal of Strategic Communication, 10*(5), 462–479. https://doi.org/10.1080/155311 8X.2016.1226172

Mohammadpour, S., Yaghoubi, N., Kamalian, A., & Salarzehi, H. (2017). Authentic leadership: A new approach to leadership (Describing the mediatory role of psychological capital in the relationship between authentic leadership and intentional organizational forgetting). *International Journal of Organizational Leadership, 6*(5), 491–504. https://doi.org/10.33844/ijol.2017.60278

Nica, E. (2015). Moral leadership in healthcare organizations. *American Journal of Medical Research, 2*(2), 118–123.

Northouse, P. (2013). *Leadership: Theory and practice* (6th ed). Los Angeles, CA: SAGE.

Walumbwa, F., Avolio, B., Gardner, W., Wernsing, T., & Peterson, S. (2008). Authentic leadership: Development and validation of a theory-based measure. *Journal of Management, 34*(1), 89–126. https://doi.org/10.1177/0149206307308913

Walumbwa, F., Wang, P., Wang, H., Schaubroeck, J., & Avolio, B. (2010). Psychological processes linking authentic leadership to follower behaviors. *The Leadership Quarterly, 21*(1), 901–914. https://doi.org/10.1016/j.leaqua.2010.07.015

Wong, C., & Laschinger, H. (2012). Authentic leadership, performance and job satisfaction: The mediating role of empowerment. *Journal of Advanced Nursing, 69*(4), 947–959. https://doi.org/10.1111/j.1365-2648.2012.06089.x

Yasinski, L. (2014). Authentic leadership: Develop the leaders within. *Journal of Operating Room Nurses Association of Canada, 3*, 36–38.